Five Days that Changed the World

Bob Chilcott

for upper voices, SATB, piano, and optional timpani

Contents

1. Thursday 29 March 1455: The Invention of Printing   3

2. Friday 1 August 1834: The Abolition of Slavery   13

3. Monday 14 December 1903: The First Powered Flight   19

4. Friday 28 September 1928: The Discovery of Penicillin   29

5. Wednesday 12 April 1961: The First Man in Space   35

Timpani part   46

MUSIC DEPARTMENT

OXFORD
UNIVERSITY PRESS

Composer's note

I wrote this piece for the Worcester International Festival for Young Singers—the first festival of its kind in Britain. The theme of the festival was peace and unity, so I wanted to find an idea that would embrace this. The poet Charles Bennett came up with five new texts identifying events that have brought people together and, by their nature, become a force for good: the invention of printing, the abolition of slavery, the first powered flight, the discovery of penicillin, and the first man in space—all things that have changed our lives for the better. The dates are as precise as can be imagined, with the exception of the date for the invention of printing (29 March), which is Charles Bennett's birthday!

The piece is written for upper-voice choir and mixed voices, but it can be performed equally well by dividing the sopranos and altos in a larger choir. The timpani part is optional.

I would like to acknowledge the Catalonian composer Antoni Ros Marbà, whose work on a similar theme, commissioned by the Catalan Children's Choirs Federation, originally sparked the idea for this piece.

Duration: *c*.15 minutes

OXFORD
UNIVERSITY PRESS

Great Clarendon Street, Oxford OX2 6DP,
United Kingdom

© *Oxford University Press 2013*

Bob Chilcott has asserted his right under the Copyright, Designs and Patents Act, 1988, to be identified as the Composer of this Work

First published 2013

ISBN 978–0–19–339008–9

Music origination by Enigma Music Production Services, Amersham, Bucks.
Printed in Great Britain on acid-free paper by Halstan & Co. Ltd, Amersham, Bucks.

*Commissioned by Sing UK for the Worcester International Festival for Young Singers (WIFYS) 2013
through the kind support of The Bransford Trust*

Five Days that Changed the World

1. Thursday 29 March 1455: The Invention of Printing

Charles Bennett (b. 1954)

BOB CHILCOTT

*See p. 46 for separate timpani part.

A programme note by Charles Bennett is available from the publisher's website.

Music © Oxford University Press 2013. Text © Charles Bennett. Reproduced by permission of the author.

Printed in Great Britain

OXFORD UNIVERSITY PRESS, MUSIC DEPARTMENT, GREAT CLARENDON STREET, OXFORD OX2 6DP

4

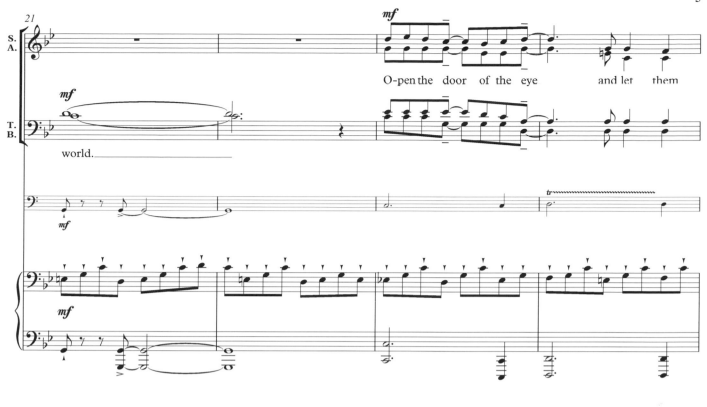

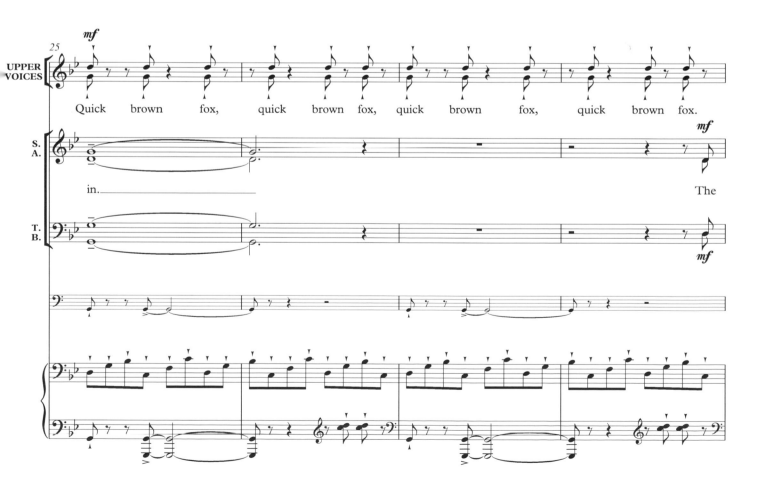

S. A.

Open the door of the eye and let them

T. B.

world.

UPPER VOICES

Quick brown fox, quick brown fox, quick brown fox, quick brown fox.

S. A.

in.

The

T. B.

*pronounced 'zed'

I knew if I took the let-ters one by one,

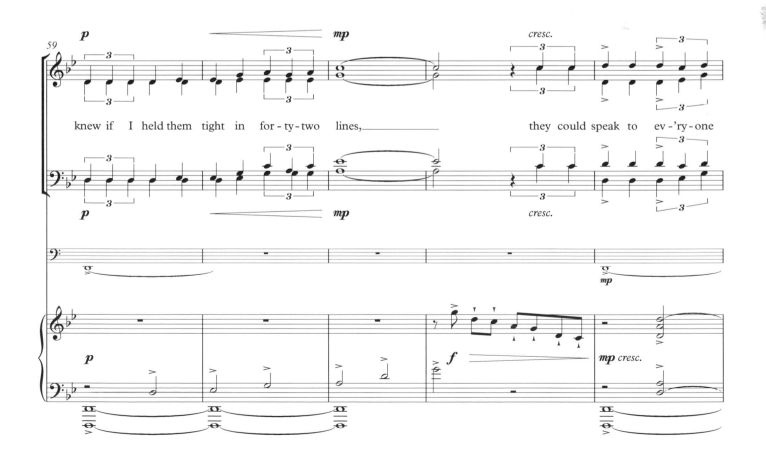

knew if I held them tight in for-ty-two lines,_____ they could speak to ev-'ry-one

ev-'ry-where, speak to ev-'ry-one ev-'ry-where, speak to ev-'ry-one ev-'ry-where._____ The

quick brown fox, the quick brown fox, the quick brown fox jumps o - ver the la - zy dog.

Quick brown fox, quick brown fox.

The foot-prints of a fox

In the be gin-ning were foot-prints o - ver the page.

who jumps

in - to your eye_ and o - ver the la - zy dog.

2. Friday 1 August 1834: The Abolition of Slavery

Charles Bennett (b. 1954)

BOB CHILCOTT

18

3. *Monday 14 December 1903: The First Powered Flight*

Charles Bennett (b. 1954)

BOB CHILCOTT

learn to fly if you give it wings.

I said to Or - ville, 'Per -

- haps.

May - be if per - haps we might

Be - low us the ground was green and hea - vy with

fail - ure. Rea - dy to break our fall. But a

thought will fly_____ some-times if you give_____ it wings. I

said to Wil-bur, 'Why not?' I said to Wil-bur, 'Why not, why____

But it pulled us up in the

end. We said to each o – ther, 'Let's

toss for who goes first.' We said to each o – ther, 'Let's toss for who goes first.' And we

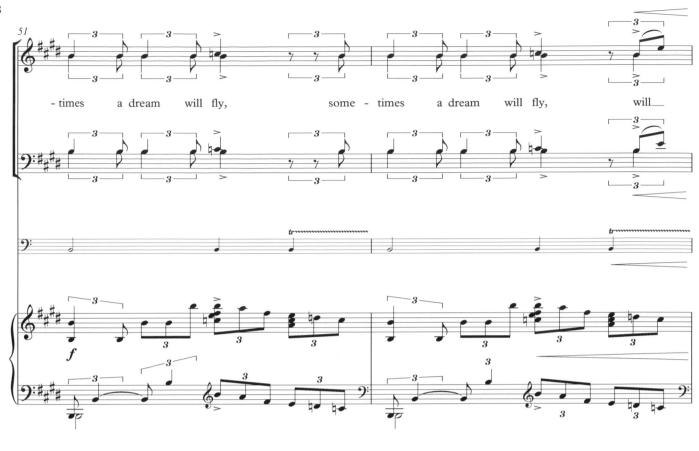

- times a dream will fly, some - times a dream will fly, will

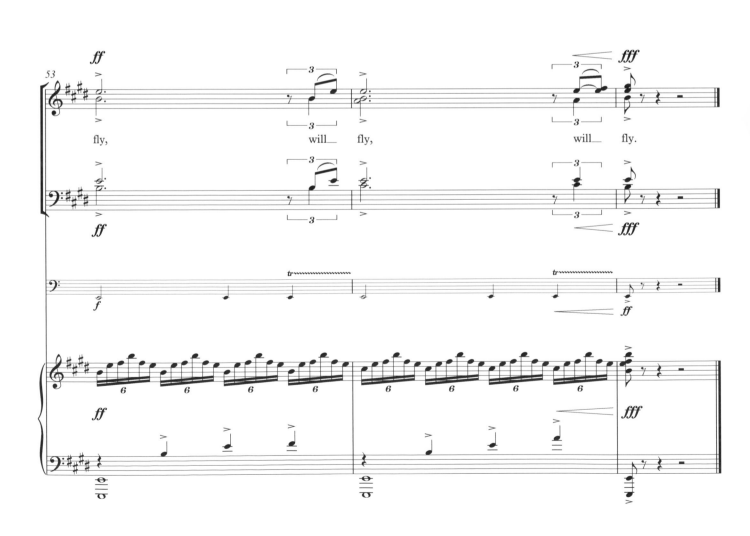

fly, will fly, will fly.

4. *Friday 28 September 1928: The Discovery of Penicillin*

Charles Bennett (b. 1954)

BOB CHILCOTT

30

32

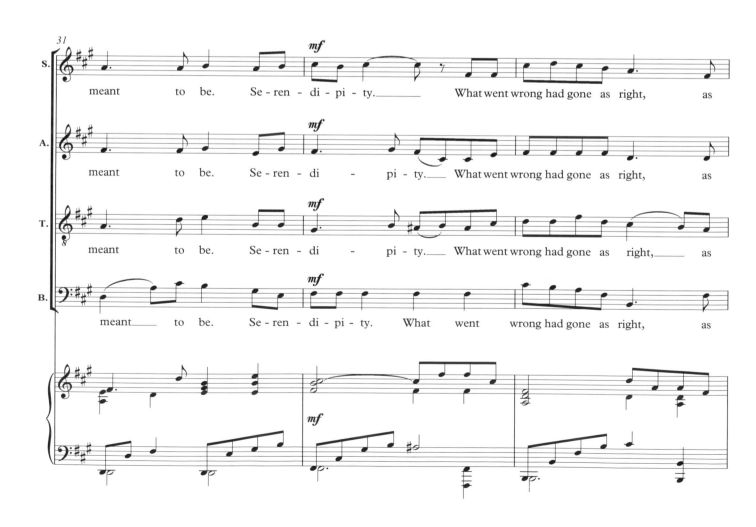

5. Wednesday 12 April 1961: The First Man in Space

Charles Bennett (b. 1954)

BOB CHILCOTT

They thought I might go mad, I might go mad._____ But I saw_ the_

thought I might go mad, I might go mad._____ But I saw_ the_ face, the

face, the face of God.

face of God.

38

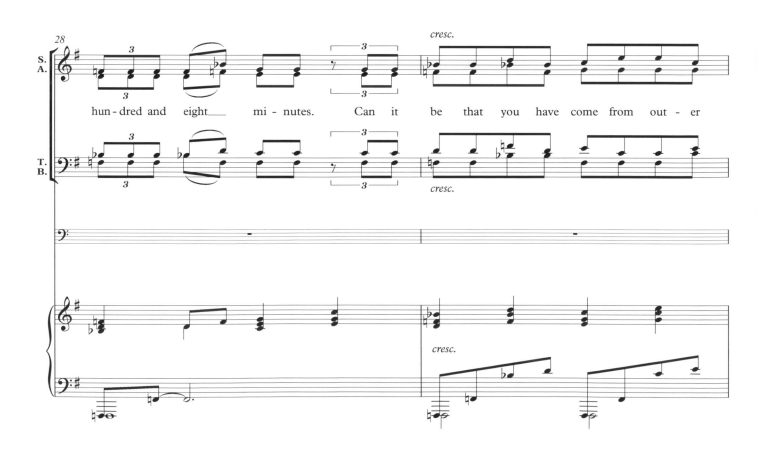

44

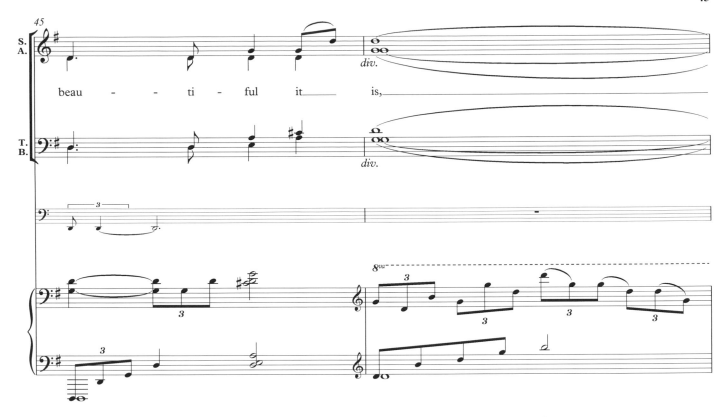

beau - - ti - ful it is,

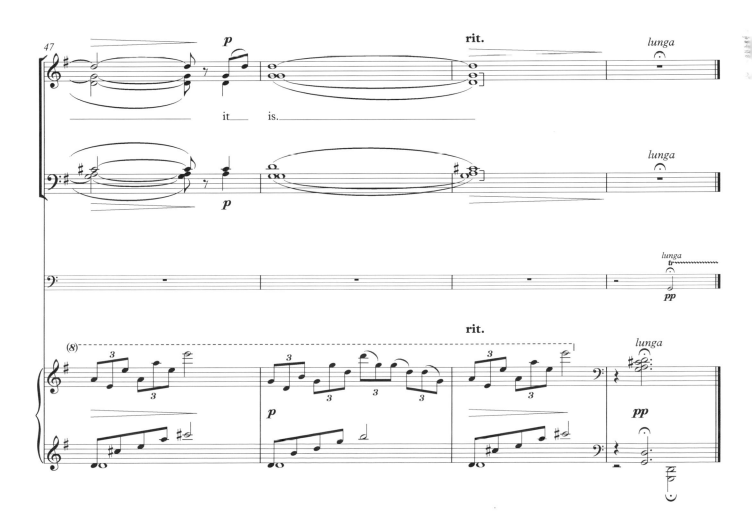

it is.

Five Days that Changed the World

1. Thursday 29 March 1455: The Invention of Printing

BOB CHILCOTT

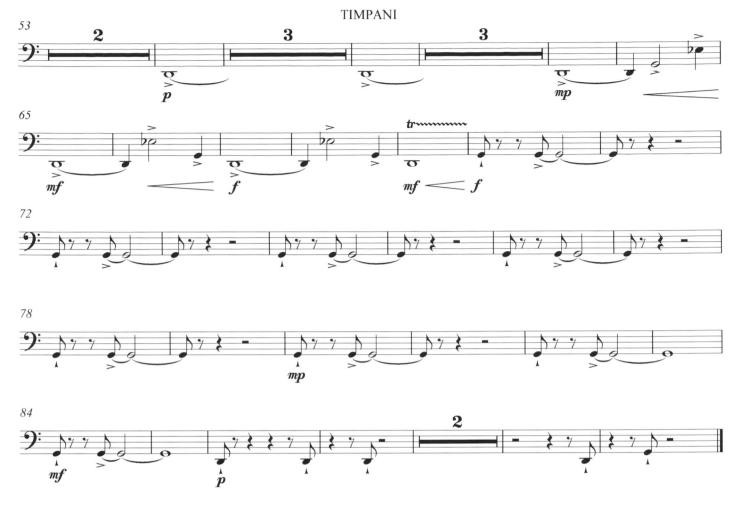

2. Friday 1 August 1834: The Abolition of Slavery – tacet

3. Monday 14 December 1903: The First Powered Flight

(time to turn)

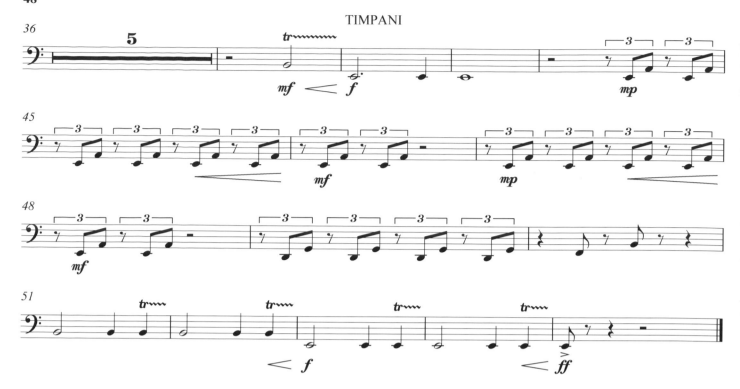

4. Friday 28 September 1928: The Discovery of Penicillin – tacet

5. Wednesday 12 April 1961: The First Man in Space

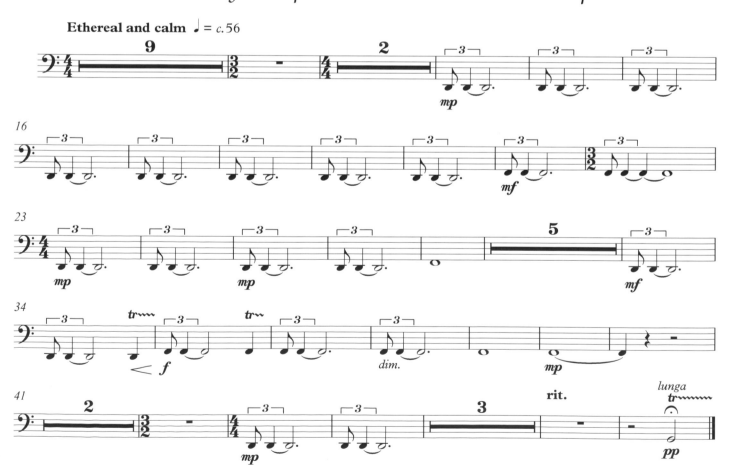

Processed in England by Enigma Music Production Services, Amersham, Bucks.
Printed in England by Halstan & Co. Ltd, Amersham, Bucks.